Temporarily
DISCONNECTED

HOW TO TURN ON THE
POWER IN YOUR LIFE

Helping Women deal with Life's Adversities

SHUNTAI BEAUGARD

ISBN: 1451504322

ISBN-13: 9781451504323

LCCN: 2010902559

DEDICATION

This book is dedicated to Helen Johnson, my mother, who gave me encouragement during my personal storm, and in memory of my dearest grandmother, Maudine Johnson, and Aunt Carol Ann Johnson.

TABLE OF CONTENTS

Inspiration

"The ultimate measure of a man is not where he stands in moments of comfort and convenience, but where he stands at times of challenge and controversy."
~Martin Luther King, Jr.

"Hope—Hope in the face of difficulty. Hope in the face of uncertainty. The audacity of hope! In the end, that is God's greatest gift to us, the bedrock of this nation. A belief in things not seen. A belief that there are better days ahead."
~President Barack Obama

INTRODUCTION

Webster's dictionary defines "intention" as a determination to act in a certain way, or what one tends to do or bring about.

Therefore, my question to you is, "What is your intention for your life?" We have the power to bring about change, act in a certain way, and do something that can make our life the best life possible, regardless of what happens in life. Intentions are something we can control. Do we intend to be positive or negative? Do we intend to live life or let it pass us by? Do we intend to be happy or sad? In any case, the decision is ours.

"Temporarily disconnected" is a metaphor. The issues, situations, or problems that we encounter in our lives are not permanent. Our telephone maybe temporarily disconnected, bank accounts may temporarily have insufficient funds, or we could be temporarily depressed, unemployed, sick, heartbroken, and even living without certain life necessities. Some may even find themselves temporarily unable to put one foot in front of the other just to get ahead in life. If we really think about it, we can intend to make those situations permanent, or we can just say:

- I am in a situation where I am currently temporarily disconnected.
- I am in a situation where right now, I feel like I can't get ahead without something pushing me back.

- It is okay to acknowledge your present circumstances.
- It is okay to have a good cry.
- It is okay to express your emotions.

However, we should not by any circumstance release those emotions to bring harm or hurt to those around us. There will come a time when we have to pick ourselves up and muster up all of our God-given strength to get out of our sorrows and go forth in our lives. On the other hand, have you become relaxed in your misfortune, hardship, or difficulty, whatever term you may use to describe your situation? Do you want to make the changes necessary to live your best life? If so, then you need not make excuses for your situations. You may ask yourself, is this woman crazy? She has not walked in my shoes to know how I feel. My response is simple. No, I may have not walked in your shoes, but I know how it feels to be at a breaking point in your life.

Fannie Lou Hamer, civil rights activist, described how I was feeling in one sentence: "I was sick and tired of being sick and tired."

I have been on my last.

I have mourned loss.

I do know how it feels when you are trying to get ahead and it feels like the world is against you.

I have had many sleepless nights wondering how I would make it.

I know how it feels to go into work knowing you did not want to get out of the bed and face the world.

What I can say is that I prayed to God that when I did finally see the light at the end of the tunnel, I would reach back to help others. I would inspire others as my mother inspired me. My mother showed me that it was okay to cry and give myself a pity party. However, she did say that after you do that, you need to make a plan and pray to God for strength.

I invite you to be inspired by how I was able to reconnect the power in my life. Now, I am able to wake up in the morning, look myself in the mirror, and be proud of my accomplishments, no matter how big or small. This book is proof that you too shall overcome, that this too shall pass, because your situation is the result of being temporarily disconnected.

Inspiration

"I'm sick and tired of being sick and tired."
~Fannie Lou Hamer

"When one door of happiness closes, another opens; but often we look so long at the closed door that we do not see the one which has been opened for us."
~Helen Keller

CHAPTER ONE:

EVALUATING YOUR DEFINING MOMENT

Viewpoint: Evaluating Defining Moments

At some point in our life, we may have encountered a moment that changed the way we see ourselves, family, friends, co-workers, or just people in general. It could have even challenged our world perspective or religious beliefs. In any case, that moment can be referred to as "a defining moment." People experience different degrees of defining moments. These moments have the potential of complicating or even simplifying our lives. Sometimes, people can't accept the truth of a defining moment, so they disregard the signs and continue doing business as usual. For example, the friend that calls you in the middle of the night with a sense of urgency, needing help or complaining about the indiscretion of his or her significant other, again. I'm sure this person may have had a defining moment but chose to ignore it. I'm just trying to keep it real. The transparency of a defining moment should never be ignored because it gives us a glimpse of truth or even the motivation to do better with our lives.

My Journey

In the fall of 2006 around the same time the color of the leaves began to change, so did my life. My grandmother, whom we affectionately referred to as Madear, was diagnosed with a terminal illness, and it completely devastated our family. Shortly after her diagnosis, I remember being in the mall at the jewelry counter when I noticed a pendent with the inscription "Love the life you live! Live the life you love!" It was at that moment that I begin to reflect on my life. I was at a point in my life where I was living it but not loving it. My marriage had experienced many problems and I was no longer happy. Later that fall, I announced to my husband that I wanted a divorce.

My defining moments were news of my grandmother's illness and having a chance reading of an inscription on a pendant. The truth about how I was feeling had always been there. The writing was on the wall a long time ago. I just chose to ignore it. See, I use to be that person calling in the middle of the night crying the same song over and over again. However, it was those defining moments that brought clarity and understanding to my situation. I could finally read the writing on the wall and take action to "love the life I live and live the life I love."

WORK IN
PROGRESS

How to Evaluate Your Defining Moment

Instructions: make sure you have some private time alone for reflection. Take your time and try to answer the questions honestly.

1. Have you experienced a personal revelation or a moment of clarity with yourself or someone in your life?
2. Please describe your experience.
3. How did it make you feel?
4. Did the revelation change your life perspective? If so, describe.

HELPFUL TIPS

Be authentic.
Stay focused.
Think for yourself.
Don't let anyone define who you are.
Keep a journal of your thoughts.
Regularly review goals and priorities.
Schedule personal time for yourself.
Remember every action has a reaction.
Don't be impulsive. Think before you react.
Think with your mind, speak from your heart.

Reflection

Think about the questions or statements made in this chapter. Use this time to express yourself in your thought journal.

Key points to consider:

- Give further details about your defining moment.
- Explore feelings about your current situation.
- Love the life you live, live the life you love. (What does that mean to you?)

Inspiration

"Faith is the strength by which a shattered world shall emerge into the light."
~Helen Keller

CHAPTER TWO:

FINDING YOUR INNER STRENGTH

∽

VIEWPOINT: FINDING INNER STRENGTH

I have found that my values, life experiences, and world-views all shape who I am. You may have picked up this book because you're dealing with challenges in your life. This book represents the beginning of your personal journey to "living your best life." Therefore, it's important for you to develop yourself by finding out about yourself. You'll discover things about yourself you never knew existed. I will challenge you to ask yourself questions and think about your life. This is an opportunity to find your inner strength. Everyone has inner strength. It's just a matter of finding it. Sometimes it takes someone asking us the simple questions, or a significant change taking place in our lives, to make us realize our inner strength. There may be things we're naturally good at, which can be strength. However, the inner strength is that something that ignites your spirit brings a sparkle in your eyes and most of all makes time stand still.

MY JOURNEY

I had a dream some friends and I were ice skating on a lake. The lake was crowded with people but everyone was having a good time. I remember hearing the laughter of children and feeling the rays from the sun on my skin. It was a good feeling. Suddenly, the happy sound of children's laughter turned into screeching cries for help. Several people had fallen through the ice. I was paralyzed with fear. The crowd began to run towards the shore for safety. A brave group of people began rescuing the victims from the cold and frigid water. Unfortunately, after several attempts, they couldn't save a little girl from the ice. So, everyone had given up and began to solemnly walk towards the shore line. I stood there in awe. I couldn't believe everyone had given up. I shouted, "We can't give up! We can't stand back and watch her die! She needs our help!" Without much thought of my own safety, I ran towards the hole in the ice and began to pound on the ice. Then I took off my coat and jumped into the ice water. I couldn't see the girl in the dark water but I managed to feel the bottom of her boot. I pulled with all of my strength and was able to pull her frozen body next to mine. Somehow we made it out of the water and I gently placed her on the ice and began CPR. A gasp of water was released from her little body as she struggled to breathe. She was alive.

I dreamed about this story after trying unsuccessfully to figure out my inner strength. I realized after this dream that I was trying too hard. Sometimes the answer is right in front of you. This dream was symbolic because it presented my inner strengths.

1. I am passionate about what I believe in.
   a. I believed the girl could be saved.

   b. I tried to involve others in my passion.

   c. I didn't let fear stop me from taking action.

2. I get great satisfaction from helping others.

   a. I had to do something; I couldn't stand back and accept the fact that the little girl was dead.

   b. I felt a sense of duty; once the girl began to breathe, I felt my job was done.

3. I am willing to take risk. I was willing to step outside of my comfort zone. Never before have I done the following:

   a. Ice skated.

   b. Ventured out on a frozen lake.

   c. Performed CPR.

   d. Challenged a crowd.

   e. Risked my life for what I believed in.

WORK IN PROGRESS

How to Find Your Inner Strength

Read the following questions and statements. Try your best to answer each question. If you're not able to answer the questions in one sitting do the following: relax, meditate, and trust me; it will come to you. Remember, the answer to my questions came in a dream.

1. Make a list of your weaknesses.
2. Make a list of your natural strengths.
3. What makes time stop for you? (what ignites you?

Was there a difference between your natural strengths and what makes time stop for you? If so, explain.

HELPFUL TIPS

Do something you enjoy every day.

Nourish your passion.

Focus on your strength; don't stress over your weaknesses.

Develop your strengths (classes, practice, invest time).

Be honest with yourself.

Be patient.

Learn to relax.

REFLECTION

Think about the questions or statements made in this chapter. Use this time to express your thoughts and do the following activities:

- Throw away the list of your weaknesses. The goal is to focus on your strengths.
- Put away the list of your natural strengths. It's good information. However, it may not be your passion. Just because someone is naturally good at math does not necessarily mean they want to be an accountant.
- Post the list of what makes time stop for you in a visible place to serve as a daily reminder. Try to focus on developing yourself in at least one of those areas. You'll find that your life will begin to transform.

Inspiration

"Do not judge and you will not be judged.
Do not condemn, and you will not be condemned.
Forgive and you will be forgiven."
~Luke 6:37

"Without forgiveness, there's no future."
~Desmond Tutu

CHAPTER THREE:

GETTING OVER IT

VIEWPOINT: GETTING OVER IT

Sometimes people do things that are stupid, irresponsible, or even detrimental to themselves and those around them. Their careless actions can quickly change or destroy a relationship. It can be easy to be unforgiving or resentful towards the individual behind the action. However, it's even harder to forgive and go on with our lives. We must learn that in order to really live our best life, there are some things that we must get over. The process for getting over things may involve forgiveness. However, the act of forgiveness is complex, and it involves more than just saying "I forgive you". Too often, we say it but don't actually do it. Then we find ourselves lost on our journey because we're looking in our rearview mirror (past) for direction. If we're constantly looking in the rearview mirror, we miss the road in front of us. If we're not watching what's in front of us, we find ourselves on a crash course destined for a collision. So, at some point, we have to stop along the way and seek new directions or, better yet, find a new itinerary.

My Journey

Webster's dictionary defines "presence" as the fact or state of being present; immediate proximity in time or space; someone or something that is present.

Today, I received a phone call from my father, a man that has not been present most of my life. A man that has not been in close proximity to give me a hug, encouraging words, protection, or love. He had no presence in my life.

When I was around nine or ten years old, I admired my dad. He was, by any standard, a handsome black man; he was tall with a well-kept afro, smooth brown skin, and physically fit. I could definitely see why he was my mother's first love. During the first ten years of my life, we had a great father/daughter relationship. We spent a lot of time together watching basketball games and fishing. I especially remember him taking me fishing. He would laugh at me because I was scared to put the worm on the fishing hook. I remember him saying, "Girl, you can't call yourself fishing if you scared to hold a worm." I was by no means a tomboy. I hated to do anything that would require me getting too dirty. On one of our many fishing trips he taught me how to drive a truck.

On that particular trip, he sat on the passenger seat of his truck and let me have the wheel. I was doing a good job driving along the winding dirt road leading away from the lake. However, caught up in the excitement, I pressed on the gas a little too much, and we were headed straight for a tree. My father took control of the wheel and told me to let up on the pedal. He said, "You must have a lead foot. It'll be a while before I let you drive again," and we both laughed. There was a feeling of security being in the presence of my father.

Those happy moments would eventually be replaced with a sense of resentment and empty promises. I visited my father the weekend of my eleventh birthday. On that weekend my father borrowed my birthday money and promised that he would give it back to me before the weekend was over. It was an empty promise because I left my father's home that weekend without my birthday money. My mother was furious with my father after learning what happened. A few weeks later, through an acquaintance, she found out my father was on drugs. He eventually lost his home, cars, job, and the admiration of a daughter that loved him so much. Over the years I hadn't seen much of him. He had moved from state to state. Eventually, his health had begun to fail because of the years of drug abuse.

So, it was not uncommon to only hear from him once or twice a year. Sometimes, several years would pass before I heard anything.

So, to pick up the phone and hear his voice was a surprise…He was trying to make amends. He was trying to be present in my life. All the hurt and disappointment buried deep inside of me came rolling out through my tears. I knew he was still my father but I was having a hard time accepting his apologies. I had to ask God to help me deal with this because I couldn't do it on my own. Regardless of my father's drug use and the devastation it caused to our relationship, I needed to forgive him. I could no longer be imprisoned by the resentment and hatred in my heart. I could not be his judge. I had to forgive in order to get over it and go on with my life.

WORK IN PROGRESS

How to Get Over It

1. Identify the source of discomfort.
2. Figure out what can make you feel better about the situation.
3. Talk to someone about your feelings (friend, family member, clergy, and counselor).
4. Surround yourself with positive people.
5. Offer forgiveness.

Helpful Tips

1. Face the issue.
2. Don't obsess about it.
3. Don't hold your baggage too long (the load gets heavier when you become tired).
4. Healing happens when you no longer feel pain from the memory.
5. Recognize your feelings (it's okay to be mad).
6. Avoid taking your pain out on others.
7. Don't blame yourself.
8. Realize you can't change what happened.
9. Talk about it with someone close to you.
10. Express yourself in the thought journal.
11. Find it in your heart to forgive.
12. If you can't forgive, talk to a professional.

REFLECTION

Think about the questions or statements made in this chapter. Use this time to express yourself. Where would you like to go from here? What is needed to make your life better? What now?

Inspiration

"The Lord himself goes before you and will be with you;
he will never leave you nor forsake you."
~Deuteronomy 31:8

"When someone you love becomes a memory, the
memory becomes a treasure."
~Author Unknown

CHAPTER FOUR:

DEALING WITH LOSS

Viewpoint: Dealing with Loss

To feel loss does not necessarily mean to experience death. Loss can be experienced due to an unfortunate outcome in your life. Sometimes, things happen that are outside of our control. However, we shouldn't let those outcomes permanently affect us. These women have experienced the following losses:

- Sandy suddenly lost her husband; he had a heart attack.
- Nicole lost her home in Louisiana because of Hurricane Katrina.
- Marie lost her job because General Motors downsized.
- Candy lost her breast; she had a double mastectomy because of breast cancer.
- Carolyn could no longer afford the payments on her home. She lost it in a foreclosure.

It's okay to feel shock, sadness, anger, guilt, or even fear towards a loss. Your feelings are valid; you're human. However, the most important thing to remember is that you're not alone, even if you feel like it.

My Journey

Today is my aunt's birthday. Happy Birthday, Aunt Ann! I tightly close my eyes trying to visualize her smile. Retrieving the past is almost like replaying an old movie or looking through a photo album. If only my mind worked like a DVD player, I would only have to press rewind, then play, to get back to any moment in my life.

Our lives are like a series of snapshots frozen in time, each photo documenting who we are and how we lived, loved, and connected to those around us. Family, friends, associates, and strangers all play various roles in our lives. No matter how big or small the role; they all have an effect on us.

Some people enter our lives for a brief moment, others for a lifetime. Certain episodes in our lives force us to think about our own life and its purpose. What is our life's mission? What legacy will we leave behind? It is my recollection of transition and the generous gift of life that my aunt left behind through her legacy that has made an impact on my life. However, it would not be until after my aunt peacefully departed from my life and the lives of others who loved her dearly to go home to be with the Lord that I realized this remarkable gift. Now, I sit here to write about her legacy and influence in my life.

My aunt had always enjoyed life; she was definitely the comedian in the family and her practical jokes were legendary. I remember being around eight or nine years old when I became a victim of one of her many practical jokes. One day she called our house disguised as a police officer. She had me convinced that a student in my class filed a complaint because I was being mean. As the conversation progressed, I was certain that I would be going to the slammer. I started to plead for my freedom, and at that point she burst out in laughter and I could barely understand her words as she uttered, "April fools."

There I was with this relieved but foolish look on my face. It was at that moment I realized even children could not escape her sense of humor.

Aunt Ann always found humor in the strangest situations; she even managed to joke about her cancer. Hair loss is a common side effect from chemotherapy. My aunt joked about how her hair was so kinky and thick that even chemo could not make it fall out. It is amazing how she continued to smile even though her health had began to decline. I daydreamed that she was a leading woman acting in a dramatic role. It would be her last but most challenging role in this so-called movie of life. She had to comfort her family the only way she knew how, through laughter.

The cancer was progressive, it began to weaken her body, and the doctors suggested that we take her home in the care of hospice. The family gathered around her and the mood was gloomy. It was at that moment my aunt had begun to make lighthearted conversation. We reminisced about the past and, before long, everyone was in tears from laughter. She had discovered that the prescription to life was to "Live the life you love, love the life you live," and a little dose of laughter can achieve the impossible. It can make you temporarily forget about your problems.

In order to deal with the loss of my aunt, I had to come to terms with my own life. My aunt lived her life in a way that brought her happiness and fulfillment. This is why she was able to comfort those around her even in the midst of her misfortune. I came to the realization that I had to make some changes in my life because I didn't feel comfortable in my own skin.

My discomfort was a result of being a voyeur to my own life. I was crippled by the "what ifs" and paralyzed by the "I can'ts. Thanks to my aunt, I realized I needed to live each day as if it were my last, treasure every moment, and remember to laugh. Therefore, I am taking a deep breath and jumping out on faith. I also know that I shall not and will not be alone in my journey, nor will you. Deuteronomy 31:8 is a verse that gives me strength: "The Lord himself goes before you and will be with you; he will never leave you nor forsake you." Those words are now a comfort to my soul because I know my aunt was never alone in her journey. Family surrounded her while, unbeknownst to us, she reached up, God reached down, and he serenely guided her home.

WORK IN PROGRESS

How to Deal with Loss

1. Take care of yourself.
    a. Eat healthy.
    b. Exercise.
    c. Allow time for yourself.
2. Don't ignore the loss.
    a. Talk about your loss with trusted family or friends.
    b. Remember the positive.
3. Find comfort in your faith.
    a. Prayer.
    b. Meditation.
    c. Counsel with clergy.
4. Make small goals.
    a. Today I will…
    b. Tomorrow I will…
    c. Next week I will…
5. Be creative.
    a. Do an art project.
    b. Journal about your feelings.
    c. Write short stories.

Helpful Tips

Don't ignore it.
Face your fears.
Allow time for healing.
Express yourself (through journaling, writing, art, etc.).
Don't be afraid to talk about it.
Remember, a dose of laughter is the best medicine.
Surround yourself with family and friends.
Be positive.
You're never alone. Lean on your faith.
Don't paralyze yourself with "what ifs" or "I can'ts."

Reflection

Think about the questions or statements made in this chapter. Use this time to express yourself. Think about your situations. Now complete the thoughts below:

What if I...
Why did I...
I can't...
I could have...
They could have...
We should have...
Why would...?

Free yourself from the negative thought. Now begin to think positive thoughts. Complete the thoughts below:

I can do...
I will do...
I am a...
I claim...

Inspiration

"Insanity is doing the same thing over and over again expecting different results."
~Albert Einstein

CHAPTER FIVE:

REMOVE WHAT'S BLOCKING PROGRESS

Viewpoint: Remove What's Blocking Progress

When I was a child, my mother and grandmother looked forward to spring cleaning. According to them, it was a time to get down and dirty and clean areas of the house that did not normally get a lot of attention. Those areas consisted of the basement, garage, and other storage rooms. Once the pieces of broken furniture, toys, and other junk were removed from the house and put on the curb for the garbage man to pick up, the storage areas seemed more organized, smelled better, and even looked terrific.

The ritual of an annual spring cleaning can be applied to one's personal life. Sometimes we have to remove the distractions, confusion, negativity, and people that stop our progress and even block our blessings. So, ask yourself who or what is blocking your progress. Only you can answer that question. Instead of grabbing a broom, pull up your sleeves and get a pencil and paper. Now, we are about to get to work. No one said this process would be easy.

My Journey

I received a portrait of myself for Mother's Day. The portrait was created by a professional artist. The likeness is true in comparison to the actual picture referenced when creating the portrait. A few years ago I would not have openly welcomed such a gift. I was unhappy in my own skin. On the outside, I portrayed beauty, poise, and confidence. On the contrary, on the inside I was feeling unfulfilled, vulnerable, and inadequate. My world as I knew it was changing; family dynamics, home, and finances, just to name a few. It was getting harder to show strength in front of my sons, and it became increasingly difficult to keep it all together. At night, when I found solitude in the privacy of my bedroom, I would cry myself to sleep. To me a self-portrait was like a mirror. The reflection would have revealed my darkest secret; I was no longer in control of my life. I felt lost and I didn't know what to do. Inadvertently, I was stopping my own progress.

WORK IN PROGRESS

How to Remove What's Blocking Your Progress

1. What are your priorities? (what's important)
2. Is your progress being blocked? If so, by what?
3. Identify your challenges/obstacles. (Please list.)

Helpful Tips

Remove distractions, confusion, and negativity out of your life.

Trust yourself.

Be positive.

Don't let others take advantage of you.

Think with your brain and speak from your heart.

REFLECTION

Think about the questions or statements made in this chapter. Use this time to express yourself. Write in your journal or just consider your life's journey.

Inspiration

"Weeping may endure for a night, but joy cometh
in the morning."
~Psalms 30:5

"Failure is the opportunity to begin again more
intelligently."
~Henry Ford

"People don't plan to fail, they simply fail to plan."
~Unknown

CHAPTER SIX

REBUILDING YOUR LIFE

Viewpoint: Rebuilding Your Life

Webster's dictionary defines "failure" as lack of success or falling short. Most people view failure as a bad thing, which is unfortunate. The key is to view failure from a different perspective. Think of failure as an opportunity for improvement, a chance to push the envelope or think outside of the box. Yes, it's difficult to accept falling short of a goal or having to start over again. However, life is not perfect and people are not perfect. Therefore, failure is a key ingredient for success. As you're rebuilding your life, refer to the challenging things in your past as bumps in the road. Don't let them stop you.

My Journey

Have you ever watched something happen right before your eyes and really couldn't believe it was happening? I was sitting at my desk when I heard the sound of a car horn. I walked to the door only to realize a white, petite woman with long, curly blonde hair and a deep tan was pulling out of the parking lot in my Tahoe. My first thought was to yell, "Someone is stealing my car!" Instead I stood in the doorway of this busy office, with my faced pressed against the glass door, watching my car disappear before my eyes. I was full of shock and humiliation.

My truck had just been repossessed. I knew it was bound to happen. I just didn't think it would be that soon. I stood inside the doorway in disbelief. What am I gonna do? It was an awkward feeling. No one in my office noticed my car had just been taken from me, and I wanted to keep it that way. The last thing I needed was co-workers prying in my private affairs. My heart sank as tears fell from my eyes. I cupped my face with the palm of my hands; mascara painted the inside of my palms.

I knew I must look like a hot mess, so I went to the ladies room. I just looked into the mirror, trying to contemplate my next move.

I couldn't even think clearly.

As I looked in the mirror, the only thing I could do was call out his name. Jesus! Jesus! Jesus! I called on him like my life depended on it. I was like a baby crying out for her mama...I couldn't hold back the tears. My back was against the wall. I needed some type of assurance. So, I prayed to GOD for strength. I felt as if I couldn't take too much more without going off the deep end.

How to Rebuild Your Life

Please answer the following questions. Remember it's important to be true to yourself. Answer the questions honestly. In order to rebuild your life, it's important to know the "how," "what," "where," and "when."

1. What's important in your life?
2. Where do you want to be?
3. What do you want do?
4. How do plan on getting there?

Helpful Tips

Do make a plan.
Do trust yourself.
Do learn from the past.
Don't try to relive the past.
Always be positive.
Discover new things.
Make the right choices for you and your family.
Don't hold on to the past.
Picture yourself living your best life.

REFLECTION

Think about the questions or statements made in this chapter. Use this time to express yourself by writing a commitment to yourself. "I am committed to…" Complete the sentence in your journal. Be detailed.

Inspiration

"Character cannot be developed in ease and quiet. Only through experience of trial and suffering can the soul be strengthened, ambition inspired, and success achieved."
~Helen Keller

"Change will not come if we wait for some other person or some other time. We are the ones we've been waiting for. We are the change that we seek."
~President Barack Obama

CHAPTER SEVEN

EMBRACING CHANGE

VIEWPOINT: CHANGE WILL COME

I watched President Obama give the State of the Union address in January. He campaigned on the premise that change was needed. However, I noticed that once he was elected president, everyone thought the change would be immediate. Sometime we get in our heads that if change is not instant, it won't happen. In his speech, President Obama stated, "I never suggested that change would be easy, or that I could do it alone." I believe that this can be applied to one's personal life. You can't make changes without the support of those around you, and change does not happen overnight; it's a process that takes work. In addition, I believe you have to be ready to embrace change. How can you embrace something you don't believe in? If you really believe change is possible, you need to prepare for it by investing time, changing attitudes, and most of all putting aside fear.

My Journey

"Don't worry 'bout a thing, every little thing gonna be all right." That's a verse from Bob Marley's "Three Little Birds." I can honestly listen to this song and understand that eventually, everything will be all right. I wish I had always thought that way. Sometimes life happens, and it can be an enjoyable voyage or a treacherous expedition.

After my divorce I started to experience severe stress. Everything that could possibly go wrong went wrong. All of a sudden I was unable to keep up with the mortgage, my truck had been repoed, and I was trying to raise three teenage sons, all while keeping a smile on my face. I was masquerading around like I had it all together. That was the furthest thing from the truth. See, I was the type of person that bottled up my feelings. By doing so, I felt like I was protecting my family and keeping myself from looking vulnerable.

Ironically, all of my so-called protection had an adverse reaction on my health. One summer night I woke up in sheer panic. My heart felt like it was about to jump out of my chest, and the muscles on the left side of my face began to twitch. Thinking it was the result of a bad dream, I went back to sleep. The next morning I woke up with numbness and a sensation that the left side of my face was drooping. It scared the mess out of me. I later found out after visiting my doctor that I had Bell's palsy, a condition brought on by stress. Keeping things bottled up inside with no escape can wreak havoc on the body. I needed to make change in my life, and I already knew the process would not be easy.

How to Embrace Change

1. Look at the big picture.
   a. Envision the change.
   b. Write down your vision.
   c. List the necessary steps to make it happen.
2. Focus on the positive.
   a. Remove negativity.
   b. Surround yourself with positive people.
   c. Look at the glass as half full instead of half empty.
3. Prepare for change.
   a. A change in attitude changes behavior.
   b. Invest time in the change you want to see.
   c. Set boundaries.

HELPFUL TIPS

Don't worry.
Being emotional about change is normal.
Embrace the change as an opportunity.
Take risk (growth is about going outside your comfort zone).
Change does not happen overnight.
Fear is like glue; it keeps you stuck in one place.
Small steps are considered progress.

REFLECTION

Think about the questions or statements made in this chapter. Use this time to express yourself. Write in your journal or just consider changes that are happening or need to happen in order to live your best life.

Inspiration

"The big secret in life is that there is no big secret.
Whatever your goal, you can get there if you're
willing to work."
~Oprah Winfrey, *O Magazine*

"The future belongs to those who believe in the
beauty of their dreams."
~Eleanor Roosevelt

"If you're walking down the right path and you're willing
to keep walking, eventually you'll make progress."
~President Barack Obama

CHAPTER EIGHT:

LIVING BEYOND
THE DREAM

Viewpoint: Live Beyond the Dream

Don't let anyone tell you not to dream. Dreams produce the most fabulous ideas because in our dreams we see ourselves living up to our full potential. The challenge is taking a dream and making it a reality. Come on, my dreamers…it's time to start living beyond the dream. Let's get out of dream mode and prepare to live our "best life."

My Journey

Three years ago I couldn't imagine what my future would bring. I had many goals. However, life happened and those goals turned into dreams. Now, several years later, I sit here in reflection, listening to Miles Davis, writing about my journey.

My heart is full of joy and my eyes with tears because I finally did it. I started out on a journey that has mentally and physically taken me to places I've never thought I would go. I've cried because of uncertainty and worried because I didn't know what to expect from day to day. In the same journey, I became a stronger woman, completed my Bachelor of Arts degree, and in the process turned this journal into a book. I'm living the life I had only dreamed about.

My hope has been renewed and my life rejuvenated. The vision for my future began with a dream. When I wrote it down, it turned into a personal commitment, and when I put it into action, it transformed my life. Along the way I learned anything is possible if you just believe.

How to Live Beyond the Dream

Setting Goals

Preparation: Think about everything you dream about doing. Don't think about it as being silly or unrealistic. The purpose is to get it out, then sort it out.

1. Visualize your goals (can you see yourself doing them?).
2. Define your goals. Take a pen or pencil and write them down. Please be as detailed as possible. (It's one thing to say them; to write them down makes them real.)
3. Don't set yourself up for failure (start small to go big).
4. Take another sheet of paper and add the following timeline:
   a. Three months
   b. Six months
   c. One year
   d. Three years
   e. Five years
5. Review your list. Prioritize your list within the timeline. Verify if your goals fit realistically within your timeline. Remember, don't set yourself up for failure. Make sure your goals are attainable.
6. Planning is useless without execution. Commit to what you want by putting it in action. Place your list where you can view it daily. That way you're constantly reminded of your commitment.
7. Share your goals with family and friends. Their support can be valuable.

8. Remember, life happens. The timeline should be fluid. It's okay if things happen in your life; just rework it.
9. Develop a personal mission statement for your life. This will give you daily inspiration.

Helpful Tips

1. If you can't envision success, you'll never feel success.
2. If you never believe it's possible, no one else will.
3. It's one thing to say it, but it takes courage to do it.
4. Think yourself happy. Don't depend on others to make you happy. They should be able to add to your happiness.

Reflection

Think about the questions or statements made in this chapter. Use this time to express yourself. What's your plan? How has this book affected your life? Do you feel it's possible to live a life you love? Describe how you feel at this moment.

THE PROCESS OF TURNING ON THE POWER IN YOUR LIFE

1. Evaluating defining moments gives life clarity.
2. Finding inner strengths leads to discovering life's passions.
3. Getting over the past gives the future more focus.
4. Dealing with loss is a process.
5. Removing challenges or obstacles makes room for progress.
6. Rebuilding your life is a chance to start over more intelligently. Think of it as a do-over.
7. Embracing change is embracing the future.
8. Living beyond your dream keeps you in reality.

Inspiration

"I had to make my own living and my own opportunity...
Don't sit down and wait for the opportunities to come;
you have to get up and make them."
~Madam C. J. Walker

"It's easy to be independent when you've got money. But
to be independent when you haven't got a thing—that's
the Lord's test."
~Mahalia Jackson

Inspiration

"I knew that whatever I set my mind to do, I could do."
~Wilma Rudolph

"The greatest gift is not being afraid to question."
~Ruby Dee

SPECIAL THANKS

I would like to thank God for giving me the strength to work on this book, and a special thanks to my sons, Richard, Xavier, and Major, for cheering me on throughout this whole process. Also, thanks to Reginald, Tosha, Carlotta, Kim, Aunt Violet, Stephanie, Evie and Phyllis for listening to all of my ideas and offering great advice. Lastly, I would like to thank my family, the Johnson family, for being supportive.

About the Author

Shuntai Beaugard is a life coach with a focus on empowering women to overcome life's adversities. She believes that "ordinary women" can become "phenomenal women" if they believe in themselves and trust in God. Shuntai uses her personal life experience to inspire other women to achieve their goals and plan for the future. She is a graduate of Spring Arbor University with a bachelor's in management and organizational development. Shuntai is pursuing a graduate degree in family life studies. She resides in Flint, Michigan, with her three sons, Richard, Xavier, and Major.

For more information about life coaching and seminars, visit: www.re-connectmylife.com.